# Science Alive!
# motion

**CRABTREE**
Publishing Company
www.crabtreebooks.com

## How to use this book

Each chapter begins with experiments, followed by the explanation of the scientific concepts used in the experiments. Each experiment is graded according to its difficulty level. A level 4 or 5 means adult assistance is advised. Difficult words are in boldface and explained in the glossary on page 32.

# Crabtree Publishing
### www.crabtreebooks.com

PMB 16A, 350 Fifth Avenue,
Suite 3308, New York
New York 10118

612 Welland Avenue,
St. Catharines, Ontario,
Canada L2M 5V6

**Published in 2002
by Crabtree Publishing Company**

Published with Times Editions
Copyright © 2002 by Times Media Private Limited

Series originated and designed by
**TIMES EDITIONS**
An imprint of Times Media Private Limited
A member of the Times Publishing Group

Coordinating Editor: Ellen Rodger
Project Editors: P. A. Finlay, Carrie Gleason
Production Coordinator: Rosie Gowsell
Series Writers: Darlene Lauw, Lim Cheng Puay
Series Editors: Oh Hwee Yen, Lek Hui Hui
Series Designer: Loo Chuan Ming
Series Illustrator: Roy Chan Yoon Loy
Series Picture Researcher: Susan Jane Manuel

**Cataloging-in-Publication Data**
Lauw, Darlene.
　Motion / Darlene Lauw & Lim Cheng Puay.
　　p. cm. — (Science alive)
　Includes index.
　Summary: Simple text and experiments describe and demonstrate the principles of motion and include a presentation of Newton's three laws.
　ISBN 0-7787-0558-7 (RLB) — ISBN 0-7787-0604-4 (pbk.)
　1. Motion—Experiments—Juvenile literature. [1. Motion.
2. Motion—Experiments. 3. Experiments.]
I. Lim, Cheng Puay. II. Title.
　QC133.5 .L38 2002
　531'.11'078—dc21

2001042424
LC

**Picture Credits**
Marc Crabtree: cover; Archive Photos: 7 (top), 11 (top), 23; Bes Stock: 6 (bottom), 10 (top), 14, 18 (both), 22 (both), 30, 31; Hutchison Library: 6 (top), 7 (bottom), 26, 27; Photobank Photolibrary Singapore: 1; Pietro Scozzari: 10 (bottom)

Printed and bound in Malaysia
2 3 4 5 6—0S—07 06 05 04 03

# INTRODUCTION

Why do we fall forward when the bus driver brakes suddenly? How can a tiny bullet pierce through a solid piece of wood? How do you send a rocket into outer space? These questions relate to motion. Motion is an object's ability to move. Learn all about motion by reading and doing the science experiments in this book.

# Contents

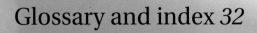

# Why do some objects move and not others?

Have you seen magicians pull a tablecloth out from under a set of dishes and wondered why the dishes stayed in place instead of crashing to the floor? It is because of **inertia**. These experiments show you how inertia works.

Difficult — 5
— 4
Moderate — 3
— 2
Easy — 1

**You will need:**
- Five checkers
- A smooth, flat tabletop
- A ruler

## Shorten the pile!

**1** Find a table with a smooth surface. Make sure there is no tablecloth on it.

**2** Build a pile of five checkers. Stack them up in a straight column.

**3** Now get ready for the action! Take the ruler, lay it flat on the table and QUICKLY slide it across, knocking the lowest checker away. The other four checkers should stay in place.

# You too can be a magician!

Difficult — 5
— 4
Moderate — 3
— 2
Easy — 1

**You will need:**
- A block of wood
- A strip of paper
- A smooth, flat tabletop
- A ruler

**1** This next experiment is a little more difficult than the previous one, so be careful! First, find a tall block of wood with a flat bottom. The height of the block should be about five times its width.

## WATCH OUT!

Do not try this experiment with breakable objects like glass. You might cut yourself!

**2** Cut a strip of paper that is wider than the block.

**3** Place the wood on the paper near the edge of the tabletop, as shown on the right.

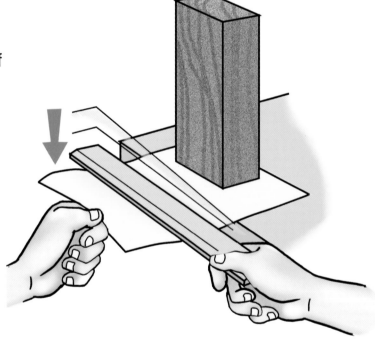

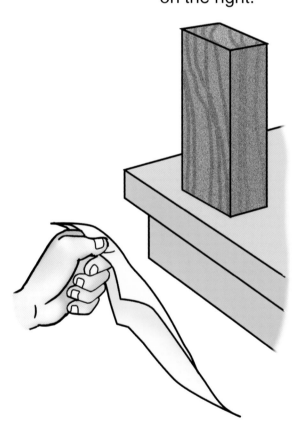

**4** Hold the loose end of the paper with one hand. Then swing the ruler down quickly, striking the paper between your hand and the edge of the table. *Presto!* The block of wood remains standing, while the paper is pulled away.

**5** After some practice, try this experiment with a taller block of wood or a plastic mug filled with water.

# What is inertia?

All objects have a natural tendency to remain still or keep moving at the same speed. This is the law of inertia. If you roll a ball down a slope, it will continue to move until its inertia is overcome by a greater force. This greater force, called **friction**, slows down the motion of the ball. Similarly, to make a **stationary** ball roll, you need to apply a force stronger than its inertia. In this case, the inertia comes from the ball's **mass**. One way to overcome the ball's inertia is to kick it. If the kicking force is not strong enough, the ball will stay in its position and not move.

Can you figure out how magicians perform the trick of pulling a tablecloth out from under the dishes? The answer is simple. When the cloth is removed quickly, there is not enough force to overcome the inertia of the dishes. That is why the dishes do not move.

A car also has inertia. It is a large and heavy object, so a lot of force is needed to overcome its inertia and make it move. This force comes from the engine, which starts the car and keeps it running.

Besides a ball and a car, can you think of other objects that need a force to move it? Where does the force come from?

# Who discovered inertia?

Galileo Galilei (1564–1642), an Italian astronomer and physicist, first introduced the idea of inertia in the 1600s. Sir Isaac Newton, a British scientist, later made it into one of his laws of **physics**. Galileo imagined a perfectly smooth ball on a perfectly smooth slope. He said if you could remove friction, the ball would quickly roll down the slope. To make the ball go up the slope, it has to be pushed or pulled, or have a force applied to it. If there was no friction, a ball rolling on a flat, slippery surface would not stop on its own.

### Did you know?

Galileo was born in Pisa, Italy. The leaning tower of Pisa, one of the seven wonders of the world, is located in Pisa. To prove a theory, Galileo was once rumored to have dropped a cannon ball and a wooden ball from the tower. Of course, the rumor was not true. The balls would have been too heavy to carry up the tall tower!

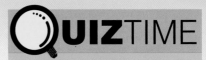

The heavier the object, the more inertia it has. Of the five objects below, which one has the most inertia? Draw a line to match each object with the number on the right. The number 1 means the least inertia, and the number 5 means the most inertia.

| | |
|---|---|
| **Car** | 1 |
| **Ball** | 2 |
| **Train** | 3 |
| **Straw** | 4 |
| **Table** | 5 |

*Answer: Straw, ball, table, car, train*

## REDUCE AIR POLLUTION!

A car driving against the wind uses up a lot of energy. The engine produces this energy by burning gasoline. Burning gasoline produces poisonous gases, and this makes the air unclean for breathing. One solution to this problem is to streamline cars. This reduces the friction between the car and the wind. As a result, less energy is needed to move the car, and less gasoline is used.

# Help! I can't stop moving!

Have you ever fallen off your seat when the bus driver suddenly slammed on the brakes? Do you know why people fall off their seats? Why not do an experiment to find out!

Difficult – 5
– 4
Moderate – 3
– 2
Easy – 1

**You will need:**
- A piece of cardboard
- A small coin
- A small toy car
- A thin book
- A thin wooden block

## The flying coin

**1** Find a room with a hard floor and no carpeting. With the book, prop the cardboard at about 30 degrees to the floor.

**2** Place the coin on the roof of the toy car. Let the car roll down the cardboard slope. When the car slows to a stop, the coin should still be on the roof.

**3** Now, place the thin wooden block about 1 foot (30 cm) in front of the cardboard slope. Check that the coin is still on top of the car, then let the car roll down the slope. What happens to the coin when the car knocks into the block? It flies off the roof of the car!

Do you know why the coin flew off the car? All moving objects have a force known as **momentum**. Both the car and the coin had momentum. When the car hit the wooden block, the force that stopped the car did not reach the coin. Momentum kept the coin moving and shot it off the roof of the car. Now try another experiment!

Difficult — 5
— 4
Moderate — 3
— 2
Easy — 1

**You will need:**
• Two rulers, each 6 inches (15 cm) long
• Five coins of the same value
• Double-sided tape

# More flying coins!

**1** Find a smooth, flat surface like a table or floor. Set the two rulers parallel to each other. Leave a gap large enough to place your coins. Tape the rulers to the table.

**2** Lay the four identical coins in a row between the two rulers. Arrange the coins so that they are about 1 inch (2.5 cm) from one end of the rulers.

**3** Place another coin in the gap between the two rulers.

**4** Aim for the center of the coin closest to you, then with your finger, flick it toward the row of coins. *Wham!* The coin at the end of the row flies off while the other coins just shift a little.

**5** Vary the strength with which you flick the coin. See what happens. With enough strength, you can even move two coins at once. Try it!

# What is momentum?

Momentum is the force which keeps moving objects in motion. According to Newton's law of inertia, a moving object continues to move unless stopped by a force. A moving object loses its momentum and stops when blocked by another object.

Momentum can be transferred from one object to another. What happened in the experiment *More Flying Coins*? When you flicked one coin against the others, the coins that were hit moved while the coin that was flicked stopped. Momentum was transferred from the moving coin to the stationary ones, causing them to move.

When traveling at the same velocity, a small car *(above)* has less momentum compared to a large truck *(below)*.

The formula for calculating momentum is:

## Momentum = mass x velocity

Mass refers to the amount of **matter**, or substance, in an object. Unlike weight, mass does not change under different forces of gravity. An astronaut floating in space has the same mass as he does standing on Earth.

**Velocity** is the speed of a moving object. The heavier the object, the more force or momentum is needed to bring it up to a certain speed. To reach 80 miles per hour (130 km per hour), a heavy truck requires more momentum than a small, light car.

# The father of motion

Sir Isaac Newton (1642–1727) was a British mathematician and scientist who discovered many laws of physics. As a child, Newton loved to invent things such as windmills and clocks. At sixteen, he went to Cambridge, a prestigious British university, to study math and geometry. A year later, Newton was sent home because of the plague, a great illness that swept through Cambridge and killed many people. Despite the interruption of his schooling, Newton continued to study at home and made many discoveries. He studied how forces changed the motion of objects and discovered what he called the three laws of motion: inertia, momentum, and action-reaction, in 1666. Newton died on March 20, 1727, at the age of 85. Many people think he was a genius.

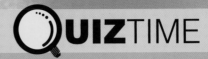

## QUIZTIME

Which ball has a greater momentum: the one rolling down a steep slope or the one rolling down a gentle slope?

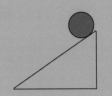

*Answer:* The ball rolling down a steep slope, because it gains more velocity.

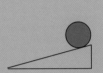

### Did you know?

Why do movie stunt people fall from great heights and not get hurt? They protect themselves by wearing heavy padding! The heavier the person, the less speed gained. The heavy padding slows down the fall, and therefore reduces the force of impact. Similarly, a bullet can pierce a hole in the wall because it is very light and gains a lot of speed and momentum!

## SEAT BELTS CAN SAVE YOUR LIFE!

Sitting in a moving vehicle without buckling your seat belt is dangerous. In a collision, your body will not stop moving forward even though the vehicle has stopped. The seat belt can prevent you from being thrown forward and hitting your head on the dashboard. Even though most cars have air bags to cushion you during a head-on crash, it is still safer to wear that trusty seat belt!

# Push and be pushed...

Have you seen a balloon flying around a room when air escapes from its open end? This is an example of Newton's third law of motion: every action has an equal and opposite reaction. Try this next experiment!

Difficult — 5
— 4
Moderate — 3
— 2
Easy — 1

**You will need:**
- A large styrofoam tray
- A pen
- A ruler
- Scissors
- Four pins
- A balloon
- A straw
- Tape
- A smooth floor

## Rocket car

**1** On the styrofoam tray, draw a rectangle 5 inches (12.5 cm) long and 3 inches (7.5 cm) wide using the pen and ruler. Draw four circles of equal size on the board. Cut out the rectangle and circles using the scissors.

**2** Secure the center of each circle onto the board with a pin. These circles are the wheels of the "car," so don't pin them too close to the board. Make sure they can rotate freely.

**3** Stretch the balloon by pulling and releasing it a few times. Slip the end over one end of the straw. Secure the mouth to the straw with tape. Seal it tight so that the balloon can be inflated by blowing through the straw.

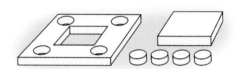

**4** Tape the straw to the car.

**5** Blow into the balloon and pinch the straw to hold the air in the balloon. Set the car on the smooth floor and release the straw. Now watch the car race away!

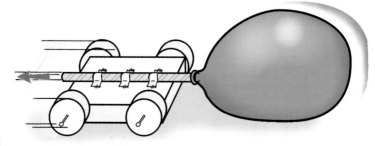

12

The next experiment is really fun!
Ask an adult to help you.

**Ask an adult for help**

| | |
|---|---|
| Difficult | 5 |
| | 4 |
| Moderate | 3 |
| | 2 |
| Easy | 1 |

**You will need:**
- A large pop bottle
- A pocketknife
- Two straws
- Tape
- Baking soda (sodium bicarbonate)
- A large tub of cold water

# Gas-propelled speedboat

**1** Using the pocketknife, cut away the top half of the bottle. Leave the cap on.

**2** Fold one end of the straw and seal it tightly with tape. Fill the straw with as much baking soda as you can through the other end. Leave this end of the straw open.

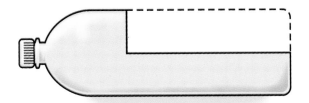

**3** Tape the straw securely to the bottom of the bottle, halfway along the bottle's length.

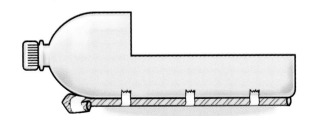

**4** Place the bottle in the large tub of water, and watch the bottle speed off! Tape another straw with baking soda to the bottle and see if it moves faster!

CRAWFORD COUNTY LIBRARY SYSTEM
201 PLUM STREET
GRAYLING, MI 49738
1-989- 348-9214

# Newton's third law

Newton's third law of motion states that for every action, there is an equal and opposite reaction. In the experiment with the rocket car, the deflating balloon forced air out, which exerted a force. This force pushed back on the balloon, making it move in the opposite direction. The car was then pulled along by the balloon.

In the second experiment, *Gas-Propelled Speedboat*, the baking soda reacted with water, producing a gas. This gas exerted a force which pushed the bottle back, making it move in the water. In both experiments, the force exerted by the air or gas (action) traveled in one direction, while the object moved in the other direction (reaction).

# The law of action-reaction

Archytas, a Greek mathematician, first demonstrated the law of action-reaction in 360 B.C. He filled a hollow **clay pigeon** with water and hung it over a fire. Heating the water produced steam, which escaped through the holes in the clay pigeon. As it escaped, the steam pushed back on the clay pigeon, causing it to move on its own.

Sir Isaac Newton expanded this law. His theories made it possible to send rockets up into the sky. This, in turn, made space travel possible.

## QUIZTIME

Rockets cannot increase their traveling speed in space because there is no air in space for them to push off. True or false?

*Answer: False. Rockets can increase their traveling speed and push off in space. This is because they burn fuel, producing gases to push them off. These gases push in the direction opposite the one the rockets move in.*

A rocket liftoff. Look at the trail of fire! The fire produces gas, which pushes downward (action), while the rocket shoots upward into the air (reaction)!

### Did you know?

According to a Chinese folktale, a man named Wan-Hoo tried to propel himself into the sky using rockets. He tied a chair between two horizontal stakes and placed 47 rockets beneath the chair. Then he ignited all of them! Guess what happened? The rockets did not burn evenly and could not lift him up. Wan-Hoo was lucky, because the rockets could have burned his chair and him with it!

## ROCKETS: GOOD OR BAD?

Rocket technology has improved greatly over the years. Today, astronauts can travel to the moon. It is also possible to produce powerful missiles that can travel across the globe to an exact location. When used in war, these missiles are very destructive!

# Why is a wet floor so slippery?

Wet floors are slippery because of reduced friction. Friction is the resistance objects face when moving against each other. When the floor is wet, there is less friction or resistance, which makes it easier for you to slip and fall. Try this activity to learn which surfaces create more friction!

Difficult — 5
— 4
Moderate — 3
— 2
Easy — 1

**You will need:**
- A small block of wood
- A stick
- Sand
- Soapy water
- A measuring tape

## What's my resistance?

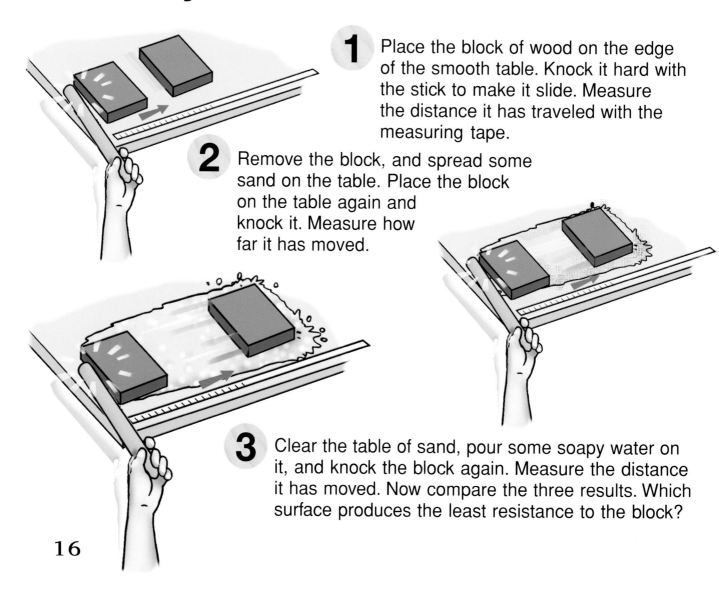

**1** Place the block of wood on the edge of the smooth table. Knock it hard with the stick to make it slide. Measure the distance it has traveled with the measuring tape.

**2** Remove the block, and spread some sand on the table. Place the block on the table again and knock it. Measure how far it has moved.

**3** Clear the table of sand, pour some soapy water on it, and knock the block again. Measure the distance it has moved. Now compare the three results. Which surface produces the least resistance to the block?

To move an object, the frictional force must first be overcome. The extra work needed to overcome the frictional force gives off heat. This next experiment shows how heat is produced.

Difficult — 5
— 4
Moderate — 3
— 2
Easy — 1

**You will need:**
• Two dry sticks

# Burning sticks!

## WATCH OUT!

After rubbing the sticks together, the surfaces will be very hot. Be careful when touching the sticks where they have made contact. Do not burn yourself!

 Find two sticks of about the same size in your backyard or a park. Make sure they are completely dry.

**2** Holding the ends of the sticks firmly, rub them against each other as hard as you can. After 20 rubs, carefully touch the surfaces you have been rubbing with your finger. Can you feel the heat?

# What causes friction?

Friction occurs because of the tiny grooves and ridges on the surfaces of objects. As objects rub against each other, these grooves and ridges snag on one another, slowing motion. The strength of such frictional forces depends on the surfaces in contact. Rough surfaces, such as sand, produce greater friction because they have more bumps, compared to a smooth surface like soapy water. This is why the wooden block traveled a longer distance on the soapy table, and moved a short distance on the sandy one in the *What's My Resistance?* experiment.

All objects have some resistance. In fact, under a **microscope**, even smooth and slippery surfaces appear rough! If there was no friction, objects would not stop moving.

Lubricating a wheel with oil reduces friction, making the wheel easier to turn. (*See the explanation on page 19.*)

The wheels of rollerblades produce little friction because they are very smooth.

# Friction and lubrication

Friction is important because without it, walking would be impossible! Friction allows our feet to push against the ground without slipping. Brakes also use friction to slow down a moving vehicle or machine.

Moving parts of cars and machinery wear down due to friction. This reduces the useful life of these parts. The excess heat generated by friction may also melt these materials, causing machine parts to stick together.

**Lubrication** is a useful way to reduce unwanted friction. This is done by coating the moving surfaces with slippery substances such as oil or **graphite.** These substances fill the tiny grooves on the surfaces, making them less bumpy and rough. Lubrication also reduces the heat generated when two surfaces rub against each other.

## QUIZTIME

Rank each object according to the amount of friction it will produce if you moved it across a dry floor. (Hint: The amount of friction depends on the force or weight of the object on the floor. The greater the weight, the greater the friction.)

1. Bucket of water
2. Cupboard
3. Brick
4. Bathmat

*Answer: 2, 1, 3, 4*

**Did you know?**
Disc brakes use friction to slow down a moving car. Rubber pads are clamped onto the discs to which the wheels are attached. When a driver brakes, the discs become glowing hot, and can reach temperatures higher than 1,112°F (600°C). The amazing thing is, they remain intact and do not melt!

## WATCH THAT SPARK!

Striking metal objects such as heavy iron tools against each other can sometimes produce sparks. It is the friction between the two heavy surfaces that causes these sparks. This can be extremely dangerous when the surrounding air easily catches fire, or is **combustible**, such as in underground mines. The ignited sparks can cause big explosions!

# Why do moving bicycles stay upright?

**B**icycles stay upright because their wheels are **gyroscopes**! What is a gyroscope? Try these experiments to find out!

Difficult – 5
– 4
Moderate – 3
– 2
Easy – 1

**You will need:**
- A bicycle wheel
- Two small cardboard tubes
- A swivel chair
- A friend

## Why does the wheel stay upright?

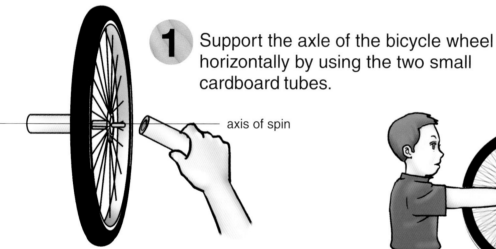

axis of spin

**1** Support the axle of the bicycle wheel horizontally by using the two small cardboard tubes.

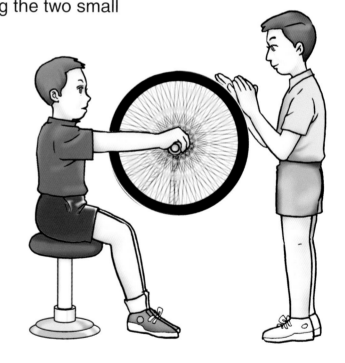

**2** Sit on the swivel chair with your feet slightly off the ground. Ask your friend to spin the wheel as fast as possible.

tilt the wheel down toward the right

**3** Now tilt the wheel down toward the right. What happens? Instead of moving in the direction of the tilt, the wheel, still upright, will turn, not downward to the right, but *sideways* to the right! The swivel chair also turns to the right! Try tilting the wheel in the other direction.

The next activity is another example of strange behavior in a spinning wheel. This time the wheel seems to defy gravity!

Difficult — 5
— 4
Moderate — 3
— 2
Easy — 1

**You will need:**
- A small bicycle wheel
- A thin nylon rope about 3 feet (1 m) long
- A friend

# The amazing floating wheel!

**1** Tie the rope to one end of the axle of the wheel. Have your friend hold the other end of the rope at eye-level, arms outstretched in front.

**2** When the wheel is not spinning, it will flip over and lie sideways. Hold the wheel upright, get it spinning, and then release it. What happens? The wheel remains upright, as if it is floating beside the string!

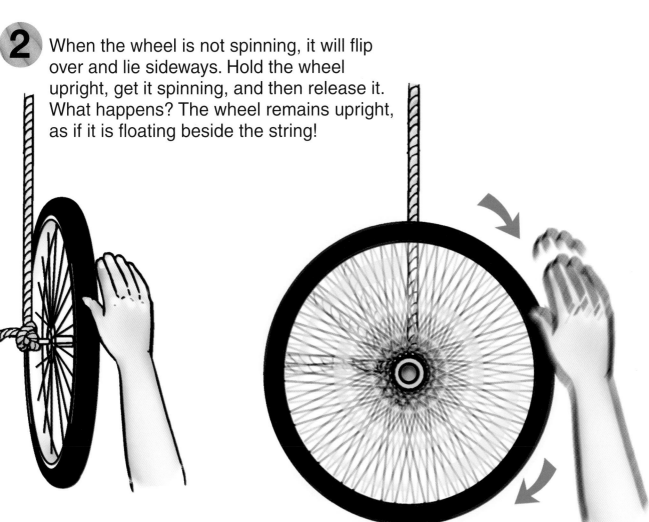

# How do gyroscopes work?

The mystery of the floating wheel can be explained by a phenomenon called **precession**. Instruments or toys which display precession are called gyroscopes.

Precession occurs when the **axis** of a gyroscope's spin changes. The gyroscope rotates on an axis at right angles to the direction of the force. Remember the first gyroscope experiment? When you tried to tilt the spinning wheel to the right toward the ground, you applied a vertical force. The wheel reacted by turning right, its axis horizontal and at right angles to your force. The wheel was precessing.

In the second experiment, *The Amazing Floating Wheel*, the **gravity**-defying feat of the wheel also occurred because of precession. When the wheel was not spinning, it flopped over due to the force of gravity. When the wheel was spinning, reaction forces acting at right angles to the force of gravity held up the wheel. These forces caused the wheel to stay upright and spin alongside the string. The wheel did not float by magic, but by the law of physics!

Both the speedboat *(above)* and the bicycle *(below)* have gyroscopes to maintain balance and to control direction.

# Inventing the gyroscope

Spinning tops are a simple form of a gyroscope that have been around for many centuries. Serson's speculum sextant, a gyroscopic device designed for use on ships, was first tested in 1743. The instrument looked like a spinning top with a flat mirror surface on top. The sextant was used to help sailors find the horizon when at sea in foggy or misty conditions. The name "gyroscope" was first used in 1852 by the French scientist Jean Bernard Leon Foucault (1826–1864; *above*) for a device that he was experimenting with.

**Did you know?**
Researchers have made a computer mouse that does not need to be attached to a computer. The wireless mouse uses a gyroscope and **radio frequency** that allow it to be used in the air like a pointer. All you need to do is point the mouse directly at the computer to move the **cursor**.

## USEFUL GYROSCOPES?

Gyroscopes have many important uses. Boats and ships often use gyrostabilizers. In rough seas, gyrostabilizers keep boats afloat. Aircraft also use gyroscopes and gyrocompasses to navigate and determine their position to the horizon. Gyroscopes and gyrostabilizers help to balance aircraft and boats, making sea and air travel comfortable and safe.

# Vrroom, away we go!

What is speed? In physics, speed describes how fast an object is moving. Try this exercise the next time you travel in a vehicle.

Difficult – 5
– 4
Moderate – 3
– 2
Easy – 1

**You will need:**
- A street map
- A notebook
- A pen
- A watch

## Calculating average speed

**1** Using the scale on the street map, calculate the distance of your journey from home to school.

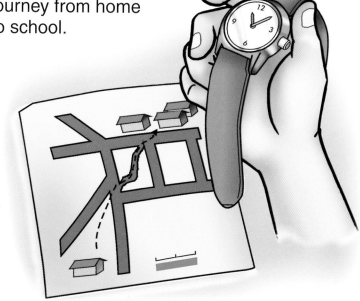

**2** Time the journey from the moment you start to the moment you stop.

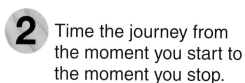

Home
30 minutes or 1/2 hour
School

1:10        1:40

$$\frac{2\text{ miles}}{1/2\text{ hour}} = 4\text{ miles per hour}$$
(7 km per hour)

**3** Divide the distance by the time taken. This is the average speed of your journey. Try this again when you travel to other places and compare the results. Do you always travel at the same average speed?

Another interesting project is a road traffic survey. You can find out if the average speed of vehicles on the same road varies at different times of the day.

Difficult – 5
– 4
Moderate – 3
– 2
Easy – 1

**You will need:**
- A road map of the survey area
- Two notebooks and two pens
- A friend
- Two digital watches

# Road traffic survey

**1** Using the map, decide on the stretch of road you want to survey and measure its length. Using the map scale, calculate the distance of that stretch of road.

**2** Stand on the sidewalk at the starting point and ask your friend to stand where the survey road ends. Make sure both your watches show the same time.

**3** Both of you should note the license plate number of each car that passes along the road and the time it passes you. If it is a busy road, survey only a few cars.

**4** Do this for twenty cars at different times of the day: in the morning, afternoon, and evening.

**5** Calculate the average speed of each car. Compare the figures for cars traveling at different times of the day. Do the average speeds vary a lot?

# What is speed?

Speed is the rate at which a moving object travels. The average speed is the distance traveled divided by the time it takes to travel that distance. Within that distance, the actual speed at any moment may vary from the average speed. Therefore, the average speed assumes that the vehicle is moving at a constant speed throughout the duration of the distance traveled. The term used for speed in physics is velocity.

The speed of vehicles on land *(below)* is measured by miles per hour or kilometers per hour, while the speed of boats *(page 27)* and ships is measured in knots per hour. One knot equals one nautical mile (1,853 m).

# Speed machines!

People are fascinated by speed! Many machines, from cars to aircraft and speedboats, have been designed for greater speed. Some speed machines can even travel faster than the speed of sound in air, which is 700 miles per hour (1,126 km per hour)! The Concorde jet flew at a speed of 1,350 miles per hour (2,172 km per hour), twice as fast as the speed of sound!

Olympic runners are also speed machines. Athletes compete to break and set new record times in their races. The fastest humans can run 90 yards (100 m) in less than ten seconds!

## QUIZTIME

Which is faster, a cheetah chasing its prey or an Olympic runner?

*Answer:* A cheetah, of course! The full speed of a cheetah is 70 miles per hour (113 km per hour). In a 100-meter sprint, the time clocked by the best Olympic runner is 9.8 seconds. A cheetah takes only 6.8 seconds—three seconds faster than the runner!

**Did you know?**
The speed of light is incredibly fast, at 186,000 miles per second (300,000 km per second)! Sunlight also travels at that speed. As the sun is far away from the Earth, it actually takes eight minutes for its light to reach the Earth. The distance of the sun from the Earth is thus said to be eight light minutes away.

## DANGEROUS SPEEDS

Traveling at high speeds gets us to where we want to go in a short time. But high speeds can also be dangerous. In an accident, the risk of damage or injury is much greater if the vehicle is speeding. The momentum of our bodies is greater in a speeding car, so the force, or impact, would be greater in an accident.

# What is acceleration?

When a moving object accelerates, it means that its speed is increasing while it is traveling. In this project, you can create a simple instrument to measure an object's rate of **acceleration**.

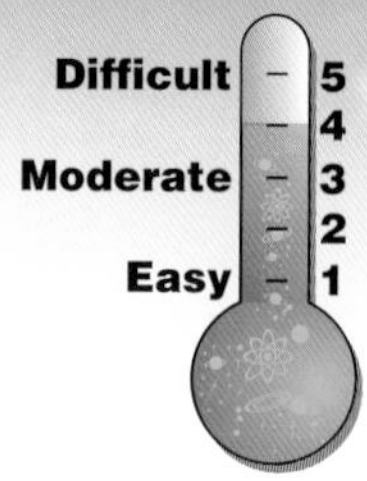


■ **Ask an adult for help**

**You will need:**

- Scrap wood
- Thick cardboard
- Wood glue
- Tape
- A strip of paper
- A ruler
- An elastic band
- A pocketknife
- A small toy truck
- A rock or weight
- A pencil
- A notebook

## Toy truck

**1** Using the scrap wood, thick cardboard, and glue, make the stand for the toy truck as shown in the diagram. Ask an adult for help.

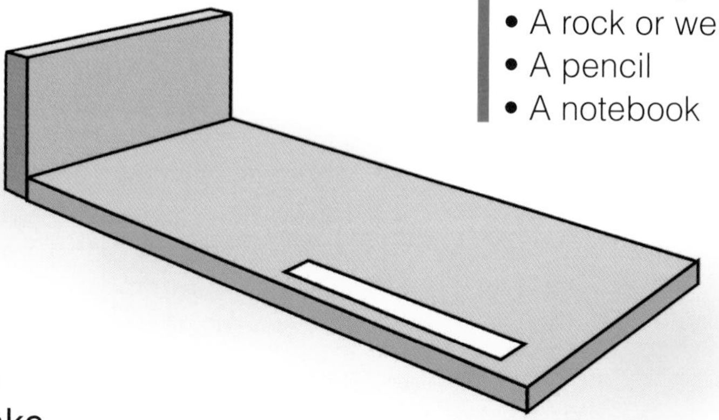

**2** Using tape, attach the strip of paper to the board to make a scale.

**3** Cut the elastic band and tie one end of it securely to the back of the toy truck. Tie the other end through a hole behind the cardboard.

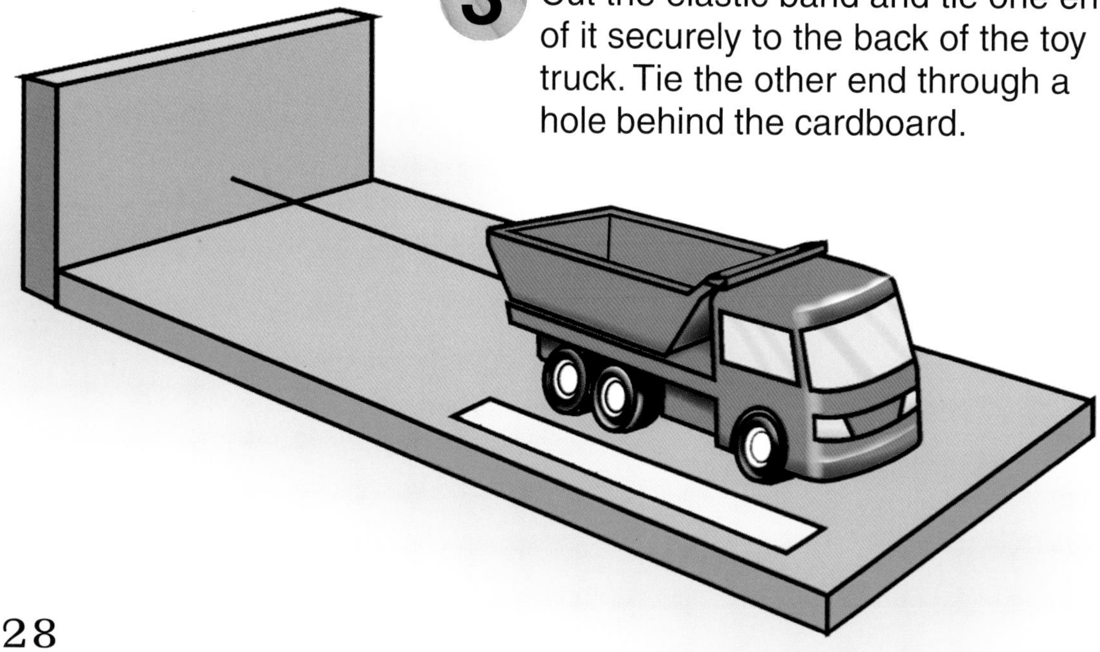

**4** Put the rock or the weight onto the back of the toy truck and tape it to the truck.

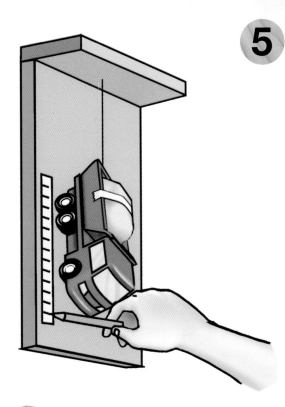

**5** To draw the scale, hold the stand upright so that the truck hangs downward and stretches the elastic band. Mark the paper scale where the front of truck hangs by writing "1.0" on it. Next, place the stand flat on a table, and mark how far the truck can reach without stretching the elastic. In front of the truck, write "0" on the paper scale. Now measure the distance between these two marks and divide it into ten equal parts. Write "0.5" at the middle mark.

**6** Take the stand into a car and hold it horizontally as you travel. The two diagrams on the right show how to hold the instrument for acceleration, or speeding up, and **deceleration**, or slowing down. The farther the truck moves along the scale, the greater the acceleration or deceleration. Write your results in the notebook. Try using this instrument in another car and compare the results!

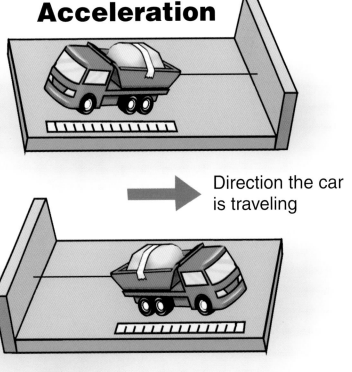

# Acceleration

Direction the car is traveling

# Deceleration

# What's the difference between speed and acceleration?

Speed measures the distance traveled over a certain time. Acceleration is the change in speed over time. In other words, acceleration tells us how fast the speed is changing. When a moving object accelerates, it is increasing its speed over a given time. For example, a car traveling at a constant speed of 50 miles per hour (80 km per hour) would be accelerating if it picked up speed to 70 miles per hour (112 km per hour). The shorter the time it takes to reach 70 miles per hour (112 km per hour), the greater the acceleration.

In physics, acceleration can have positive (+) or negative (–) values. A positive value means that the moving object is going faster, or accelerating. A negative value means that the object is going slower, or decelerating.

When a roller coaster ride starts, you might feel like you are being thrown back against your seat. That is because the sudden acceleration produces great force.

# To go faster quicker!

It might be possible for machines to reach high speeds, but faster acceleration, or reaching a high speed in a short period of time, is also important. Racing vehicles, such as the motorcycle below, are made to reach high speeds in the shortest amount of time. Faster acceleration gives an advantage over competing vehicles. In racing, *that* headstart certainly is an advantage!

## QUIZTIME

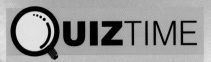

Two cars, A and B, took off from the same starting point. Car A accelerated faster than Car B in a given amount of time. Which car would be farther from the starting point after that time?

*Answer:* Car A would be farther from the starting point. Since Car A accelerated faster than Car B, it would have traveled a greater distance in that given time, compared to Car B.

### Did you know?

Not only is the cheetah one of the fastest animals on the planet, it is also capable of amazing rates of acceleration. From a standstill, a cheetah can reach 45 miles per hour (72 km per hour) in two and a half seconds! That is faster than any sports car ever made!

## USE LESS FUEL!

A launching rocket must accelerate to a certain speed to generate enough force to overcome the Earth's gravitational pull. Most of the large amount of fuel carried by the rocket is consumed during this process. To make space travel more efficient, scientists are using high speed aircraft to launch space shuttles from mid-air. This reduces the amount of fuel burned.

# Glossary

**acceleration (page 28):** Increase in speed of an object over time.

**axis (page 22):** An imaginary line that runs across the center of an object.

**clay pigeon (page 15):** A clay disc with holes.

**combustible (page 19):** Any substance that mixes with oxygen to give heat and light.

**cursor (page 23):** A symbol showing where data is being keyed on a computer screen.

**deceleration (page 29):** Decrease in speed of an object over time.

**friction (page 6):** The resistance objects face when rubbing against each other.

**graphite (page 19):** A soft form of carbon that can conduct electricity.

**gravity (page 22):** The force of attraction on objects to the Earth's surface.

**gyroscope (page 20):** A device with a rotating wheel to maintain balance and control direction.

**inertia (page 4):** The tendency of a body to stay at rest or constantly keep moving in the direction of the force.

**lubrication (page 19):** Adding a slippery substance between two surfaces to reduce friction.

**mass (page 6):** The amount of matter in an object.

**matter (page 10):** The amount of substance in a body.

**microscope (page 18):** An instrument with a magnifying lens, which makes objects appear larger.

**momentum (page 9):** The force present in a moving object. The greater the mass or velocity of the object, the greater its momentum.

**physics (page 7):** The study of matter and energy.

**precession (page 22):** The sideway motion of a spinning gyroscope when given a push to its axis of spin.

**radio frequency (page 23):** The frequency of the transmitting waves of a radio message.

**stationary (page 6):** Something that is still.

**velocity (page 10):** The speed of an object traveling in one direction.

# Index